Dr. Wain -
 One of the luxuries of
my life is having someone
like You in my life !

# Immortal Kisses

## Confessions of a Poet

I hope you enjoy many
magical moments
reading these wonderful
poems!

Love,
Pauli
@ xxx

# Immortal Kisses

## Confessions of a Poet

*By*
Mitzi Libsohn

*Arranged and Edited*
*By*
Pauli Rose Libsohn

PAGE PUBLISHING, INC.
New York, NY

First originally published by Page Publishing, Inc. 2014

ISBN 978-1-62838-598-4 (pbk)
ISBN 978-1-62838-599-1 (digital)

Printed in the United States of America

In memory of my beloved husband

David

# ACKNOWLEDGMENT

One person made these poems happen:
Pauli Rose
My quiet partner from beginning to end,
she worked around the clock for months
and burned the midnight oil.
It was she who slipped the idea for this book into my pocket,
and with her gifted skills and intuitive insights,
brought it together and gave it life.

# THE POET IN ME

Like chinks in a garden wall that are never closed up, the art of poetry is distinguished by its fissures – its narrow openings that let yet another poet in.

Set in motion by a burst of imaginative power, I am spurred on to create – impassioned by the poet in me – scattering the seeds of my imagination over the printed page. These poems, these flowers, these jewels in the sun – are produced from a vein of material that runs through the mainstream of my consciousness and from which I extract pure gold. The imagery which I paint conveys my life's experiences and like beautiful sketches seen at an exhibition – they endure – they stir the emotions – and their haunting qualities are vivid expressions of a recaptured past. It is within such a framework that I have immortalized those lines, figures, and pictures which I have sketched so vividly from memory – creating poetic arrangements and an artistic style which contribute to the lyrical beauty of the poems themselves, giving them a sense of fullness while heightening their emotional power.

In the world of poetry, there is no single ruler, no king or emperor – no queen or empress. But some poets surpass others – some produce one flower, some many. The brief period of time in which the poet functions is a definite period in time as it is related to the worth, meaning and influence of their work. The special meaning of that work may not be immediately apparent, but as it moves and passes slowly in time, its impact on our senses produces reactions and repercussions.

Mitzi Libsohn

# FOREWORD

Mitzi Libsohn has reached her destination as a poet through the individuality of her style which is inseparable from her life's experiences. The fluency – the rhythmic flow – the rich narratives – all create a oneness of artistic expression that make her poems stand apart for their striking individuality. The haunting quality and extraordinary mental images – love recaptured and lost, nature's landscapes, the moon, the endless sky, and the eternal romance of the sea – all, once penetrated, have the power and force of life. Exceptional for their lustrous quality – their radiance is a reflection of her poet's mind – producing richly embroidered tableaus woven with a common thread. Mitzi Libsohn's poems display an array of eloquent poetic artistry that have a distinction of style upon which she has placed her stamp.

Pauli Rose Libsohn

# CONTENTS

## IMMORTAL KISSES

## The Calm And Chaos Of My Garden

# Forget-Me-Nots

## COMMON AS CABBAGES - ECHOES OF MY CHILDHOOD

## POETIC ESSAYS

# IMMORTAL KISSES

# WHERE HAVE THE WILD GEESE GONE?

Where have the wild geese gone

Whose cries broke the silence

And filled the stillness of the night

When once you held me in your arms

And we listened?


Where is the moon

That floated through window panes –

Crossed and recrossed thresholds

And gave new meaning to the mysterious night

As you lay beside me?


And O my love!

Where is the unforgiving wind

That whistled and sang through eaves,

Blowing away with its songs

And settling its chill on the passion

That lay in your last kiss?

# I HEARD A BIRD SINGING

While half-asleep in the arms of my belovèd,

I heard a bird singing.

And the song flowed from tree to tree,

And the trees swooned and sang with it,

And it fell like dew on every blade of grass,

And it melted snow on mountains carved like statues.

And on this night,

It crept like a shadow where we slept,

And rested with us.

Its sweet melody rose and fell with your breathing,

And it tangled with the moonbeams in your hair.

And in the morning,

It became your voice when you wakened

And calmed me with your kisses.

# REVERIE

Gently comes the night.

Once again deathless visions that bear your traces,

Move from tree to tree,

from window to window,

Haunting the dark recesses of my mind.

And in one maddening moment,

They become you,

And all the manifestations of you

When love was strong –

Before you slipped away.


Was that your voice I heard whispering in the willow last night?

# THE APPLE GREEN DRESS

What became of the apple green dress once so dear to me?

I am wanting it again

And I am wanting the girl who ran in it

Flirting with the sea

And the gulls who surrounded her.


On a winter's night

I close my eyes and remember

How I smelled of salt

When the dress was wet.


Farewell sweet dress!

I loved you

And you never asked me why.


…'twas for your pretty color.

# MEMORIAL TO LOVE

How we loved the moon all those nights

When you cradled me in your arms

And the breath of our longing

Surrounded the swans who climbed out of the lake

To stare at us like ghosts.

And when we looked in their eyes

We saw years flooding out –

Years that never warned us that nothing lives long…

Not even the messages of love moaned low by the bullfrog

At midnight.

# IMMORTAL KISSES

Ghosts imprison'd by YESTERDAY

Stand guard and laugh

When I grow dizzy with the taste of kisses remembered

Kisses frozen in my throat

Kisses you gave me when we danced on the beach.

Immortal kisses.

# I REMEMBER JOY

I remember joy

That died like the elm

Without a cry.

Peacefully.


And I said to the dust

"Here lies love".


O what a loss!

# WHEN THE SHADOWS WERE US...

The willow raises her arms to the sky

And like an eager lover,

Whispers to an April moon.

Stars light their candles and glow with desire

Through cracks in my window.

And there behind the willow

Long shadows stand 'round

Waiting in lines like Degas dancers.

Soundlessly they fly on flying feet

Seeking your love

As I knew it yesterday

When the shadows were us

And you cared for the willow

And you cared for me.

# I WILL ALWAYS DREAD APRIL

When winter comes

(My first winter without you)

I will remember the anguish between us

When we parted in April.

Tears mixed with rain.

I will always dread April.

# THE MOON SURPRISES ME TONIGHT

The moon surprises me tonight.
Passing through a gap in my fence,
She presses a smiling face against my window
And robs me of sleep.


Why hast thou wakened me
O voiceless silent queen of a million years?
Would that I could rise on wings and winds
To live in your kingdom
Where I would be met by stars singing softly,
And a sun with golden crown and roses in her cheeks.


But what would be the good of all that?
I would look down to see my love walking in the heather
That ripples like waves of the ocean.


And I would remember how he comes
Rushing at me like the wind,
And I would remember his kisses,
And I would hasten to escape
from the smiling moon
the singing stars
and the sun with roses in her cheeks.

# WHEN I AWAKEN FAR FROM YOU

When I awaken far from you,

The rose forgets to bloom.

The lark that once sang lovingly sings now without passion,

And the voice of the sparrow is hushed.

The daisy greets me with downcast eye,

And summer leaves before its time –

When I awaken far from you.

# IMPRISONED MEMORIES

Your presence is inseparable from the willow tree,

Where, every morning,

For one miserly moment,

Imprisoned memories come out

And spring into a perfect expression of your face,

Only to recede into the nothingness

That exists behind my closed eyes.

# NIGHTSCAPE

The ululations of a racing wind have just begun.

Somehow breaking through the calm walls of my being,

They cover me with a cold blanket of dread

And tell me that the void of night has come.

The moon turns up her light and glimmers like a white eye,

And for a brief moment, I hear your voice in the wind

That blows like a tempest, wounding the trees.

Lying in darkness,

I hear the perpetual ticking of a clock

That hauntingly suggests the beating of my heart.

The night smells of a thousand roses that waken my sensuality,

And in this wretched interlude of waiting for you,

Time forever lost pulses yet

And moves in a circle with nowhere to go.

I lose my mind when it whispers in my ear

That you have forgotten my existence.

# TREES WITH MANY MOODS

I run between trees with many moods.

illumined by the moon

they are animals

illumined by the sun

they are a man and a woman

smiling

and falling in love.

# WITHOUT YOU

Tonight the moon hangs like a jack-o-lantern,

And squanders its light in a witch-black sky.

The apple trees are singing,

And a gust of wind brings the scent of apple blossoms

Into our tiny room where you lie in my arms.

Dreamlike, I think how useless the moon would be without you.

Stars would leave the sky and never return – without you.

The sun would bend its head in grief and only pretend to rise,

And I, I would close my eyes and suffocate in solitude –

Without you.

# MY PATENT LEATHER SHOES

The moon tumbled down last night

And landed on my patent leather shoes

With the silver buckles.


My how they shine!

# ...A MOMENT OF TRANSCENDENCE

In a moment of transcendence,

I watch in wonder as a glorious moon descends

And dips behind my picket fence.

My eyes feast upon its whiteness,

Which falls like an avalanche of snow

On the drooping arms of the willow.

All around, shadows scatter like flowers in a storm.

Sleepless goblins haunt the darkened landscape

And dance allegretto on the grave of long-ago lovers.

Suddenly the moon is gone, but you stand before me.

I feel your breath,

And the hundred promises you never kept

Slither and die in the dust.

I pretend to feel no pain as I sink in your arms,

Once again a slave to the kisses you spill on my lips.

# THE SMELL OF LONELINESS

I turn to face morning

And a pillow that says nothing.

The smell of loneliness drifts in through the window –

Seeking and finding me.

# ...MY DESIRE FOR YOU

I love the sound of the wind

When it sings in my ear like a bird.


I love the smell of the lemon tree

When it bows low and brushes my face.


And my heart leaps

When the pink lotus blossom emblazons the night.


Its scent surges through my senses

And stirs my desire for you.

# A LARK SINGS...

Lying in her nest,

A lark sings a lulling song pianissimo,

But it falls like thunder on my heart

When you leave with the fragrance of the wild rose

In the morning.

# WAS IT ON THE NILE THAT WE MET...

Was it on the Nile that we met

And breathed the same air in a distant arcadian age?

When your eyes open to me,

I swear they flow over with images from some other time,

Some other place.

And in a moment of mystical continuity,

I see you standing where veiled ladies

Once gathered on sands the color of shantung,

To listen under twirling parasols

As flowers and birds sang in concert

When you walked by...

# MY NIGHT WITHOUT YOU

Day turns into night.

The moon passes between the apple trees

And curls up like an old dog on my window sill

Where I rest my head and dream dreams of you.

The roses smell like a whole flower market,

And the red currants are on fire.

But the true locus of the night

Lies in the melancholy song of a meadowlark.

Calling from the deep of darkness,

Its promise of love unfurls like a wide glittering scarf

That envelops me completely

And relieves the bleakness of my night without you.

# LAMENT

The shrill cries of cicadas haunt the night,

And like a few bars of music,

Echo my longing for you.

Why oh why

Did you turn and go

When I loved you so?


Birds on the wing ask why…

Parched trees waiting for rain ask why…

And even the weary river

Scented with ancient civilization

Yes, even the river

Asks why.

# ...THE GREEN OF YOUR EYES

i never wanted to drown in the green of your eyes

or be caught between the thrill of your kiss

the sound of your step

and the beauty of the reddening apple.

# ...THE BEST PART OF OUR LOVE

Alone with the sound of your voice,

I remember how I watched you,

And even the sun glanced at you,

As you stood knee-deep in clover,

A crown of daisies in your hair.

And I reflect on all that was lost

When the wine from the fruit we had tasted ran dry,

And the daisies became oppressive –

You, with the look of winter in your eyes,

Closed the last door

On the best part of our love.

# SHADES OF NIGHT

The lyric strains of rain on the roof

Accent the softly sung song of a nightingale,

And blend with the lovelorn lament of a guitarist

In the distant wide sea of the night.

The sweet fragrance of crushed roses

So ripe… so sensuous…

Unmoored by a summer breeze,

Floods the night, soaking me in its beauty,

And I am haunted by memories not yet dead –

– of a night when the moon wore all her diamonds,

And our love was supple as a bough,

And tender as a peach.

# SUMMER GRASS

There is no sweeter grass than summer grass

When lying in the sun there is you beside me

Curled in the shape of an S.


A robin with fanned out wings

Sings a tune to her baby in a cradle of twigs,

And in my ear

That tune will become an almost masterpiece

Like your face

When you leave me in the morning,

And the village clock

Shouts that time has made a fool of us.

# ...I HEAR SUMMER'S FOOTSTEPS

Winter closes its portals

And I hear summer's footsteps rustling in the grass.

Majestic as a queen,

She comes dressed in green with yellow jonquils in her hair.

Sowing seeds and singing like a lark,

She carries the sweetest flowers I have ever seen

And lays them 'round the chestnut tree

That stands like a chimney beside her.

In the slanting sunlight,

Baby apples hang like emeralds,

And when the wind swoops down,

I hear them laughing as they fall in bright red heaps.

Creeping vines rise like enormous ladders –

Incandescent blossoms surge softly against my window

And silently turn into purple grapes so pungent,

They remind me of the bitter tears I tasted

When I fell in love with you.

# CHANSON D'AMOUR

By the light of a crescent moon,

I see my true love's scarlet lips

That brim with wine.

Chestnut eyes that gaze like goddesses

Will haunt me 'til I die.

And when she breathes,

Her breath is as a gift of incense

From the soft wood of cedar.

But I am fondest of her hair.

For when it encompasses me,

I bathe in its ripples,

And the second half of my life begins.

# ALL FOR LOVE

I lie down to sleep perchance to dream.

And if I dream I want to dream

That love is more than a dead leaf.


I will have this vision that love has no ending,

And you will come up beside me

Like a sweet little breeze on a windless day

With a kiss that travelled far from home

Far from Troy where Helen lived

And is remembered as the queen

Who launched a thousand ships –

All for love.

# ABRACADABRA!

Standing on sand that used to be shells,

I feast my eyes on the brooding beauty of the sea.

A rosy sun sits on my shoulder and listens

As a solitary sandpiper tells a pointless story

To the empty corridors of my heart.

Ghosts of memories rise out of the sea

And dance before me.

I whisper your name

And ABRACADABRA!

I behold your face under a big hat in the sunshine

Waiting to be kissed.

# ONCE UPON A BEACH

Morning!

The world is waking

And the sun with half – closed eyes is watching

Us

As we walk side by side collecting shells.

A blue green sea churns around our feet

And scatters fishy smelling foam.

A big fool of a seagull is singing

And shaking his wings.

Sandpipers dance polkas

And a crab comes out of a hole

As if to greet us.

(solemn as Socrates

why is he here?)

Astonished – you bend to touch his claw

Refusing to be afraid.


We break into laughter.

# NIGHTWATCH

Yellow as butter,
The moon closes her eyes
And drops down to slumber behind the trees.
Stars shine like silver sequins,
Making me wish they were mine.


Shadows caught in silence
Cradle memories in their arms,
And sway, I thought, like lovers
Entwined in the rapture of a kiss.


The frogs – in mock-heroic mood –
Sing a bit of opera to amuse me.


Rain on my window goes ping!
And the wind brings the smell of lime
Through a wide open door,
Creating the illusion that you are here,
For many times have I smelled this perfume in your hair
When you combed it.


You are late in coming.
Vaguely, I feel as if the world is dying.


But when you come…
O but when you come!
Time disappears
And I exult in life.

# A NIGHT WITHOUT PASSION

Late in rising

A midnight moon pokes its face into the trees

Before drowning in the lake in the park

Where strangers going nowhere

Talk in the dark

And drink from the empty cup

Of a night without passion.


Why should I care?

# WHY THIS TORMENT?

Robins romp on the grass

And are metamorphosed into you.

In exultation I turn from the nothingness

When you vanished with a final kiss.

I call and listen –

Rain falls like blows on my face.

Can I outlive this loneliness?

The robins won't tell me.

# A SPECIAL VOICE

I listen in vain

for the sound of the voice of my love

on this useless night

when he loves not me.

# THE SHAPE OF YOU

The shape of you rises in the green robe of the fern

That sways when light winds wrinkle the mouth of the river.

I listen and look for you –

The low voice of the lark tells me that you are not coming.

I hide my desire behind the willow and weep.

# CAN IT BE...

Can it be that only yesterday

The sun rose out of its bed

To warm us as we lay like cats in the high grass

Listening for sparrows

As a toad waltzed by to stare?

The mind stands poised to remember

When we were happiest

'Neath the willow all crooked with age.

Now the smell of its leaves is enough to waken dreams.

Shadows meet and sway.

Somewhere a cricket sings.

My thoughts hunt for you.

# THERE IS NO YOU

A brilliant first sun of the day

Flashes like a yellow lamp

And scatters light on some weeds

That smell like peppermint in a bowl.


A rooster squawks in the barnyard.

This is the only sound

And it chokes me

When I stumble into the past

Where all roads lead to you

And there is no you.

# YOUR EYES...

Your eyes came into being in the sea,

For they are as deep as the sea.

And you, you are a fugitive from the moon,

For you are as distant as the moon.

Yes, your eyes are as deep as the sea,

And you, you are as distant as the moon.

# SEEDS OF LILIES

On a summer night

The cold fire of a silver moon

Lights dark and lonely places in the forest

Where seeds of lilies lie cradled

Like babes between the rocks.

Watered,

They rustle and bloom

(Works of art)

Then beckon and bid us welcome

When we lie down on the grass

And close our eyes –

Blinded by the infinite incomprehensibility

Of the moon.

# ...WHEN THE LILACS BLOOMED

Snow has come.
As I sift through it
I remember a day in April
When the lilacs bloomed.


The sun was shining
And the vacant air
Came alive with itinerant birds
Settling and resettling on a carpet of leaves
As if gathering for a reunion.


Now I walk in winter
Musing on dead blossoms that surround my feet.
I hear your voice humming the river's song,
And I sense your nearness everywhere...


...in snowflakes that fall and cover my face
And in slender trees that walk like phantoms
Down paths where we once walked
When the lilacs bloomed.


Chilled –
I sink into snow,
And in one bittersweet moment,
Yesterday becomes today when you appear in the twilight –
But it isn't you.
It's a tiny sparrow unfolding its wings.

# WAS IT ONLY YESTERDAY…

Was it only yesterday
When your long, long hair
Kept uncoiling and uncoiling,
And its weight ran through my fingers like water,
And it became a tawny tiger's tail
Wrapping itself around me
As you tossed it to and fro
When you leaned over me in a pool of light?

A passing wind threw open a window
And the unrehearsed song of an unknown bird
Floated through…
Catching its rhythm,
We became a pair of dancers
Lithely leaping across a collage of silvery leaves
That softly slipped down from a willow tree,
Glinting like diamonds
As they fell on your loosened hair.

And even now…
Your presence is inseparable from the willow tree,
Where, every morning,
For one miserly moment,
Imprisoned memories come out
And spring into a perfect expression of your face,
Only to recede into the nothingness
That exists behind my closed eyes.

# WHERE ARE YOU?

I read your letter by the light of the moon

And your words make me pine for the time

When we stood in the rose garden

And you said

"look how the roses bend as tho' curious to see us!'

Tangles of roses – the color of tea.

How you fussed over them daring to call them art!

Today the smell of roses comes into my room

Driving me mad –

Where are you?

In my imagination – you are approaching.

Hurry!

# DOUBT

How mute the moon

How silent the stars

How meager your love.


I hear a night bird sing.

Some songs are all alike

But not this one.

This song keeps me company in the dark

And it is a prop against the doubt I have

That the door will open

And you will come rushing in to swear that you love me

And even the roses staring through the window

Will swear that you love me.

# ...THE TEMPTATIONS IN MY HEART

The moon is a white bird that rises

Under the black lids of the night

To be my love

And feed the temptations in my heart

Until I see you once more.

# BEFORE YOU GO...

Before you go,

Assuage me with your kisses.

Let them fall like ornaments upon my neck,

And I will taste their fragrance in the daylight

When you leave.


Before you go,

Assuage me with your kisses.

Let them flash like jewels upon my throat

And I will catch and count them like a miser

When you leave.


Before you go,

Assuage me with your kisses.

Let them rain like rubies upon my lips

And they will light the darkness on my pillow

When you leave.

# BREAKING WAVES

I close my eyes and rock with the sea

That always keeps singing.

How softly it floats in my lap!

Drifting – I become the sea

Hunting along shores in the heat of summer

For you.

# YOU COME FROM THE SEA

You come from the sea at sunset

And I see you as I have never seen you before.

Glittering in shades of blue green and gold

You glide in the attitude of a dancer

Swifter and more alluring

Than horses flying on a carousel.

# LIGHT WINGED LOVE

O light-winged love that outruns time

You live in the eye of the willow

in the cry of the loon

and in my hunger for you.


Stay with me!

Stay with me!

# I AM NOTHING

Waiting for you

I am nothing

Until I go down to the peartree

Where priceless pears drip their scent

And I am nothing

Until the clang of the garden gate

Signals that you – whom I love – are here.

# VIGNETTE

The sun is a slave to your beauty.

Curious,

She visits in the shade of the laurel

Where you lie hidden in my arms.

Birds in a row

Crow in delight

To see the sun light up the greenness in your eyes

And lay fire to the redness of your upraised lips.

# WILD SCARLET BERRIES

Do you remember
When wild scarlet berries
Split apart from the vine
And went without tears
To scatter and dance at our feet?
Blown by the wind,
They caught in your hair
Lighting it up and coating it with flame
In the sunlight.

Do you remember
When wild scarlet berries
Exploded
And sated the thirst of some plump snowbirds
(Waiting boisterously!)
Squirting juice into open mouths
And splashing fiery red liquid
That trickled in serpentine patterns
Before sinking into the cold and dusty ground?

And do you remember
Wild scarlet berries
Whose outpourings were in harmony with our own
When the scent of a sensual night
Enfolded us
As we drifted away from the rest of the world?

# LOVE ENDURES

I dreamed a dream that I was never needing you.

why then upon waking

do I find a hint of you

in the fragrance of the wet grass

in the pungence of the plum tree

and in the waiting shadows

that follow me to sing songs in your voice?

# ...I AM ME

A cock crows

The sun comes up

My dreams have gone

And I am me

Again.

# ...LOVE IS NOT A DEAD LEAF

A brilliant first sun of the day
Flashes like a yellow lamp
And scatters light on some weeds
That smell like peppermint.


I dream to the sound of crickets singing
(or is it spiders spinning?)
And this sound is the only sound
And it is the very sound
That sends a shiver down me
When I sink into the past about a million times a day
To utter your name.


I dream many dreams
And in one of them I am consumed by the illusion
That love is not a dead leaf.
And I taste happiness
When you come up beside me
Like a sweet little breeze
With a kiss that cools my cheek.

# AND SUDDENLY I KNOW...

A foot of snow has fallen.
How fragrant it is!
The willow tree, embroidered and be-ribboned in sculpted ice,
Shimmers in the moonlight,
And with a lyricism all its own,
Conveys an incandescence that outshines the moon,
And defies the bleakness of the night.
Imprints in the snow tell me that you were here,
And I can almost taste your nearness.
Blinking stars electrify the sky with cold nuggets of light.
A shrieking wind prances like a pony
And nuzzles me among the shadows.
A meadow lark appears out of nowhere touching down at my feet.
And in this landscape in which I find myself entangled
With the willow, the stars, the wind, and the lark,
They all range themselves behind me in the dark,
Assembled as if intense listeners to the litany of my memories.
And suddenly I know what they know.
–That nothing can fill the vacuum of your absence.
Not even the warm heart of the vibrant rose
That throbs beneath the snow.

# SILHOUETTES

A cold and silent moon,
Luminous in white,
Mirrors and reflects clandestine lovers
Silhouetted like dark flowers,
And shines on them as if a giant streetlight.
In the shadows,
Modigliani eyes gleam against alabaster faces,
As lithe bodies unbend and cascade downward from craggy dunes.

A midnight caravan of laughing seagulls,
Overdressed in floppy wings,
Joins them in a ring of light,
To pipe lyrical love songs that harmonize with
The impromptu pas de deux of the moving figures.
Gliding across the landscape,
They seem to grow smaller and smaller,
Until, like exiles in fabled Paradise,
They vanish in the yawning labyrinth of the night.

Stars with eyes of their own,
Gather in clusters,
And even the infinitesimal ones
Watch in fascination
As, in a reprise,
They continue their dance
In the ring around the moon.

# IMPROBABLE LOVERS

We walked along deserted shores,
You and I.
Improbable lovers squandering time,
Odd flowers waiting to bloom…
Flickering rays of the morning sun
Radiated out over meadows, mountains and all the oceans,
Until a vagrant fog rolled in,
Eclipsing everything.
Along the way,
We thrilled to the endless monologue of an invisible bird,
And danced on the roof of shifting sands,
Whose rhythms sculpted and perpetuated our footsteps.
Wavy lines of sandpipers loitering in rambling conversation,
Turned 'round on teetering legs,
To glare with blazing eyes
As we passed by.
A pair of flirting loons careened overhead,
Filling the cavernous sky with yodeling song,
Before submerging on delicate webbed feet
Into the gaping mouth of prowling waters lurking below.

And now, as a pendulum swings at midnight,
Familiar ghosts return to the nooks and crannies of my mind,
Meeting me in the dark
With a flower I cannot touch,
A voice I cannot hear,
And a pair of beckoning eyes that refuse to go away.

# A SEDUCTIVE MOON...

A seductive moon turns up her light.

Covered in liquid lace,

She sweeps across the sky searching for ghosts of other moons,

Whose last gasps I hear rumble like thunder over the desert,

Where I stand in the dust

Listening and waiting for someone like you...

# ...THIS FATALISTIC NIGHT

The moon is at my window.

How contentedly she sits on the wide sill

With no regard for the stars she has abandoned!

And with a tapping at my window,

She enters and parades past me,

Radiant in gems like some legendary empress

On her way to the throne.

Wreathed in a thousand rays of light,

She searches everywhere,

As if to find her missing lover

And draw him out of hiding for her pleasure

On this fatalistic night.

# GOLDEN—EYED DREAMS

Hush!
Rhapsodic whispers in the night
Slip through an evening fog,
Ushering in golden-eyed dreams.
Crowded with stray ghosts that intimidate me,
They melt in a mystical landscape stranded in time
Where small yellow spots pulsate,
Transporting me back to the dark side of memories.


But the sharp redolence of red roses with red roots
Lingers and vivifies my waking senses.
Opaque nectar gushes forth falling over me like water,
And in one singular moment of duality,
I am between earth and sky
In extricable linkage once more with you.


Along the periphery of my mind,
There flows a musical river
That endlessly chimes when it sings
– I remember…
– I remember…

# ...THAT YOU ARE MINE

The whippoorwill who never fails to call your name,
When will he learn that you are mine?
The wordless willow whose branch once bent to touch your face,
Now hangs its head in grief,
Because you are not there.
When will it learn that you are mine?


The untamed rose,
That dollop of red in my garden,
Whose thorn is meant to sting,
Whose petals you once plucked,
Grows drab and diminished without you.
When will it learn that you are mine?


Must the moon wither and lose its light?
Must the sun become indifferent and die
Because you left with no goodbye?
When will the sun and the moon both learn that you are mine?


As for me,
Forlorn as a raindrop without rain am I,
And sullen as a snowdrop without snow.
When will I know that you are mine?

# GLINTS OF GREEN

How to explain the changing color of my love's eyes

As she rushes to greet me?


Glints of green

Escape and flutter like birds,

To become ideal partners of an impetuous spring,

So verdant

That flowers seem more than flowers.


Dabs of iridescent lavender pulsate

And float out like murmuring whispers,

To overlap and mix with shades of purest brown

Extracted from dark shapes

That flow from the sensuous mouth of the

Sinuous

Surging

Unforgiving

Nile.

# ONCE...

Once
My love was like the wind.
Bold as a buccaneer,
Whirling about in a fury,
Howling from across valleys,
Rattling windows
Demanding to be let in.

Once
My love was like the wind.
Cold as a curse
Sighing over wet cobblestones,
Howling from across valleys,
Pounding doors,
Demanding to be let in.

Once
My love was like the wind.
Old as a moonrise,
A half-mad king with weary eyes,
Howling from across valleys,
He stroked the trees until they shuddered,
...and whispered lies
Before turning away to leave,
No longer desiring to be let in.

Left alone – I am in his arms,
And even in sleep,
I shall see my love until I die.

# THE CALM AND CHAOS OF MY GARDEN

# THE SOBS AND SIGHS OF APRIL

Winged tulips in the sky –

Birds in flight going who knows where.

Mild as sheep,

They flee undying from a speeding bolt of lightning

That smiles with jagged teeth laid bare,

And stoops to cut the crimson rose that was my ecstasy,

And stills the beating heart of the little willow

That stands by the river that flows like a snake.

I remember how birds and insects and even a toad,

Assembled to mourn the rose that pillowed them in its folds,

And they wept for the willow that was the roof

Beneath whose shade they slept.

But most of all,

I remember the sobs and sighs of April

As she surrendered to grief in a torrent of tears,

For she could not rekindle the rose or the willow

When she kissed them goodnight.

# LAST SUMMER'S ROSES

A rooster crows

And the day begins.

In the cool emptiness of the morning

I can smell last summer's roses in the fallen petals

That lie toasting in the sunshine.

Their fragrance haunts me and lingers like perfume

Hidden in an old unopened drawer.

A low-lying lemon tree quivers and sways in a sudden wind.

Endless stalks of lilies unwind

In a procession of porcelain blossoms

That seem to step out of a Japanese print.

But it is last summer's roses that are the soul of my garden,

I am wild with happiness to see them come back

As if never away…

Always red, they seem redder still,

And I suffer the pain of Cupid's arrows

When I fall in love with them again!

They will always be mine.

# FRAGMENTS

The day was cold and still

When the petals fell from the roses.

Whole clusters white as ganders and geese

Hopped and fluttered about

And I wondered what would I be without them?

Suddenly dead they moved with the wind

And came to me.

What were they?

Ladies dancing?

Love letters torn to pieces?

When I kneeled to gather them up

They lay in my arms

And shone as if lit by lamps.

# THE MOON IS A GOLDEN APPLE

The moon is a golden apple

And the stars are flickering fires.

I can smell the roses that lie brooding

In my flower-filled garden.

A song of yearning from the curved throat of a nightingale

Hangs in the air.

Reclusive violets breathe with scented sighs

Washed out to sea where sailors swoon.

A trumpeting sound from far-off trains

Soars on the wind…

Their fragility is shattered when it returns in a puff of smoke

To resonate as footfalls and whispers at my window.

# THE INCONSTANT MOON

Adrift in a dream
I see a moon with feline eyes the color of marigolds
And her face is painted with the whiteness of eggs.
Sphinx-like she walks into the night
And meets me where the willow has stood
For one hundred years.
I race to touch her but BOOM!
She is gone.
Her inconstancy evokes a sense of sadness
As when the rose petals that were my heart's desire
Withered and lay bruised and broken in the dust
Their ghosts caught in the minutiae of a frozen pond.
Or
As when the magenta flowers
That sprouted in the slits of my fallen-down fence
Bloomed in vain before I could heal them.
Imperfect were they and wild as the sea,
But in exquisite harmony with the fallen-down fence.


The willow wept when they died.

# I AM A TREE

I am a tree.
Old as the sea.
I remain alive
A paradox of power and decay.


Death bides with me
And is about to take me for his bride.


Never again will I lift mine eyes
To hyacinths and Queen Anne's lace,
Nor will I ever laugh again with lovers
Come to steal a kiss beneath my boughs.


Hark! who calls to me?
Why 'tis Death –
And here's my grave!
Quietly I go into the dust,
Not even having bled.


O pity the poor starling
Who will race to see me in the spring!
How awful her grief!
How broken her song!

# THE WIND WINDS ITS WAY...

The wind winds its way across meadows and fields in May,

Tripping on stones and walking on wheat,

It blows where an old owl sleeps

In the hollowed-out trunk of a cottonwood tree,

And lulls him with a song

That will haunt him for a hundred years.

...and even the listening lark will labor to learn it.

# WINDING TRAILS OF BIRDS

Winding trails of birds in rapid flight

Abandon unloved nests in darkened woods,

And with a thousand voices singing,

Take possession of a burgundy sky.

With the sun and the moon behind them,

And the earth and the sea below,

Undulating lines fade into black dots

That seem part of a hollowed-out woodcut.

Voyagers, obsessed with the open sky,

They embrace the bolt of lightning

That comes without warning to light their path.

Listening bodies hearken to the first echo of spring,

And in rhythm to the tocking of an invisible clock,

They return with the daffodil,

To sing their songs for me.

# NOCTURNE

I am alone with a full moon
That enters my garden
Where it stops to rest on a willow tree
Whose branches bend to touch me.


How bright the stars!
I see them gather,
Perchance to listen
When golden birds fly swiftly by
And dip beneath the moon.
The tumultuous rustle of wings
In the infinite void of the sky
Comes to me when the wind begins to blow.


And over me,
I see them flying two by two and wing by wing.
Filling the sky with song,
They make music over my rooftop.


Now where are their songs
When no song sings?
Vanished with the rainbow,
They run like raindrops
And fill the woods with lilies in the snow.

# IMAGES

Even a fool would love the moon
When pale as a pearl
It moves so languidly across the river and over the bridge!
A clock chimes twelve when it sets down to rest
In the arms of an enormous oak tree.
I tremble with joy to see its wise old face
Peering at me from under the swaying magnolia
That smells like oranges.
A pair of darling doves curled up in their nest
Sing of golden corn
And steal my heart at dawn.
A drizzle of rain washes the uncut grass
Where a thousand toadstools spring up unbidden!
To my delight,
They glisten like tiny sculptures.
And O how I love the wildness of the wind
That goes bang on the shutters.
I alone can hear it when it plays several flutes
Before flapping away with a billow and a wail
That rock my roof.

# MOONSCAPE

O moon

Come to me on wings!

You are more beautiful than the elm that weeps.

And yes!

You are more beautiful than the riddles I have seen

In the darkness of the black crows' eyes

Who circle downward in a great wide arc

To dig for worms

And to see me.

# A GATHERING OF BIRDS

Birds gather and stand beautiful as a painting

On the branches of a white oak – heads cocked –

In perfect balance with a yellow sky.

An owl hoots from the decaying trunk

Of a withered willow

And a chickadee kisses the snow's white bosom

Of a luminous weed that grows in common clay

Seeking the thrill of sunshine.

# SHADOWS OF MY CHILDHOOD

The moon is ablaze and red as a rose.

Stars are dancing not far from my window.

How I long to find a road that will lead me to them!

A tall white willow wears nothing but ribbons in her hair

And flings herself at the moon as if to reach it.

Trees in top hats are walking.

They bend and say goodnight in booming voices.

I end up feeling empty

When they disappear into the night

As shadows of my childhood.

# THE CALM AND CHAOS OF MY GARDEN

In the calm and chaos of my garden

Where so many loves have I,

Ruined roses rise up again.

Goddesses.

Flames of my soul.

Their eyes look upon me

And bid me remember

That they have come far from nothing –

Breathing ecstasy into the earth

Running like blood as they moved with the stars

To find happiness

'Neath my worn wooden fence

Where they bloom in the dark

And wait for me.

# VISIONS IN RED AND WHITE

Winter comes
And a tearful willow sobs to see the last leaf fall from the oak.
Wrapped in a mantle of snow,
She pauses to brush her long hair,
And I am aware of her standing with snowy crown
Poised like some forgotten queen
Holding court in the vacancy of the night.
The wind in a fury sifts through rotting leaves,
And with vivid brush strokes,
Paints the rosy red rose dead.
A dozen times a day
I am haunted by the tragedy of the rosy red rose
That broke away and danced off
To the violent music of an icy wind.
(The willow went mad and refused to recover).
But my heart thunders with happiness
When I behold the specter of my precious rose
Shimmering in the mist over the frozen lily pond
Now lit by a neon moon.

# WOULD THAT I WERE A BIRD!

The old chestnut tree shakes the earth

When it rises in the morning

To seize and conquer me

Like some ancient Pharaoh.


Would that I were a bird!

Small as dust

I would be a slave to its will.

O to rest in the tranquility of its kingdom

And never think of death!


I would search the sky

For the sudden flight of singing geese

And if they be gods

I would beg to be one of them

When they alight softly –

Softly like rain on crisp green grass

To dine on daffodils

And drink from buttercups.

# THE OLD QUINCE

I am obsessed with the old quince.
My dearest tree!
Stricken with age –
A flash of green and gray you are.

But O! how you used to bloom!
Blooms as far as the sun could reach –
Red blooms and blue ones too.

Silent now as if listening –
You rise on stilts among the weeds
Arching to see me
When swiftly down the path I walk
All wrapped in rings and rubies
Breathless to see you.

Tho' poisoned by ruin you beckon
Then all at once the best of what you were
Comes 'round again.
Renewed.
Untroubled.
Unweary.
And with one last breath
Branches climb the air
Then bend and sway to stroke my hair.
Tenderly – like a lover.

On the edge of passion –
We are content to be two phantoms
As we go into the night under giant stars.
Rooted in this place.
Forever young.

# YESTERDAY'S MONARCHS

In the moist golden mist of morning,

Trees bent by an autumn wind

Shiver and rise out of velvety shadows.

Yesterday's monarchs in moody meditation,

They sit on gnarled roots in hollow-eyed splendor

Haunted by visions of their own deadness.


Yearning to reach the clouds,

They arch upward –

Tilting and nodding in sweeping curves

…and in a miracle of balance

Struck between candelabra arms and tangled fingers,

They lift and pillow precious nests

From which lonely swallows sing love songs

That coalesce with the whispered music of the trees,

And the cadenced fury of the wind.

# A GATHERING OF GEESE

A meditative moon
Solemn in spectral white,
Looks down
And casts watchful eyes on
A gathering of geese.
Dormant black shadows adrift,
They wipe sleep from melancholy eyes
And come alive with trumpets blaring,
A pounding of wings
And a whoosh of unfolding feathers.
Nestled on waves of aqua waters,
They calmly float onto barren shores.
Laden with unspoken desire,
They strut and ruffle with urgent steps
And scatter to court each other,
Exchanging wide smiles and syncopated chirps.
Vibrant creatures,
Their perpetual posturings explode into spiraling flight.
Gliding geese soar like eagles,
Until the cold curved fingers of a cruel sea
Come from everywhere,
To pull them back in a violent plunge
Of splashing spray.
…The fragile flames of passion
Sputter and flicker in the moonglow
Leaving delicate traceries
That fuse with the rushing waters.

# MARCH WIND

An ornery March wind uncoils
And lashes the arms of a frail willow tree,
Sending chills up its spine
And jolting a blasé bluebird hidden in its shadow.
Swaying in the wind,
His face an unblinking mask of noble breeding,
He sings out in melting musical oration.

A small bustling beetle skitters to a stop,
And with head bent to keep the wind at bay,
Listens to the lure of the song
That blends with the beat of his own repetitious clickings.

Sailing ahead of the hurrying wind,
A sundried bunch of violets with little yellow eyes,
Becomes a feathered cap to a rollicking tumbleweed,
And bursts apart to surrender its perfume
To the loving hands of the willow
Which stands weeping in the wind.

# COPPER-COLORED BIRDS

Copper-colored birds

In fluid flight

Sail by

A white-faced moon.


(Illumined in a crimson sky,

Are these the unhated flowers of yestermorn

Disguised as candescent candles in space?)


Graceful virtuosos now,

They sing together in perfect tune.

Pulsating bugle sounds

Emerge from delicate throats

To resonate and flash like lightning,

Against the vaulted ceiling of the sky!

# A BLAZING SUN

a blazing sun sits on the green willow tree

then plunges into the rhododendruns.

even the dead weeds that should have been pruned

are lit by fire.

# FUZZY WILDFLOWERS

A surging crowd of fuzzy wildflowers,

Gaudy giants gaily teetering on gnarled stems,

Rush to greet a hint of sunshine in the morning stillness

And fondly sniff the scented air.

Their owl eyes, fit with precision in pink faces,

Turn with startled pleasure to gaze upon

A quartet of bluebirds on the wing,

Who break the calm of an empty sky

With the flute-like sweetness of their faraway songs.

# SILKEN ROBINS

Silken robins in a swirl,
Embrace a misty morning as it comes.
And in a poetic surprise that melts my heart,
I chance to see two robins feeding on a creeping vine
All bent with grapes that bleed when open
And stain my feet as I am coming up the path.


Now when the wind blows cold,
And the snow piles up to humble me,
I am lonely.
But there are the robins to think of.


…scarlet gnomes romping on the green green grass.
…red ornaments on my window sill.


I used to leave my window open wide
Hoping they would come inside.


I am not forgetting them.


What clock will chime the time
And I will stop to listen
For the rush of wings against the eaves again?

# LOONS ON THE LAKE

Eight young loons have gathered on the lake.

Their yodelings float over me before dropping like stones

In the heather that blooms waist-high at the end of the lake,

Where I lie in the shade of a nodding chestnut tree

Listening…

And when the loons are long gone,

Brittle leaves turn to rust and dance to the rhythm of October.

I begin to smell apples,

And I rush to pick my last pumpkin before the first frost.

My happiness erupts when I see a lone loon rise in the mist

Above the lake,

Only to sink a moment later when the lake washes over it,

Silently spawning an amorphous shape

That is an offering from the eight young loons

Who journeyed here in May.

# NIGHT HAS FALLEN

Night has fallen.

The moon stands poised over three sheep

In a field along the river.

Stars march their ancient march

Erasing darkness over hollyhocks

Tall and slender in my garden.

The scent of roses hangs thick

In the throat of a nightingale

Whose song washes out to the lake

Where fish jump and dazzle me with their games.

Their eyes tell me that I am never alone.

# MAYBE TONIGHT

Maybe tonight

The moon

(O deathless heroine of the sky!)

Will come to life

And lift her silvery veil

And raise her voice in sensuous solo,

And the whole sky will listen in surprise –

And even the wind, hurrying somewhere,

Will stand still

And find it hard to forget the bittersweet strains

Of the birdlike song

That permeates the sky.

# WADING BIRDS

Footfalls heard herald
A long line of wading birds.
Sensual beckoning shapes,
The commotion of their movement
Spreads like wildfire,
And roils the watery graves of forgotten life.


Crimson-faced,
Scarlet flowers that forgot to bloom,
The blaze of their procession ignites the sky.
Plumes heavy with aroma,
They zigzag about,
Seeking songs to sing.


In a torrent of flight,
The stage is set for the power of their music.
Piped arpeggios tear the sky apart
And fall like kisses on the horizon below.


How could they know
That the soul of their celestial songs
Would unite with,
And live again
In the sound of falling rain?

# PORTRAIT OF SANDPIPERS

Sandpipers stand half-asleep at high noon.

Lulled by lapping waters

They contemplate the why of being

And rock with the motion of the sea

As if it were a cradle.

# WHAT THE ROBIN KNOWS

The moon looks down

And sobs warm tears that fall like rain

On an old ruin of a tree waiting to die.

A silent robin knows what the moon has lost

And sings a mournful song beside its ashes on a hill

Where in the spring a poppy grows

And then a hundred more burst forth

To light the air –

Joyous! as if freed by death to be immortal,

They sit enthroned beside the grave of the tree

Which the moon had loved –

– Potent queens unslaughtered by the beast of time.

# LITTLE BLUE HERONS

A bewitching audience of little blue herons

Ceremoniously gathers for a princely parade.

Witty, vibrant harbingers,

They walk in satin slippers,

Murmuring sibilant sounds.

Their sighs mingle with glances

From smoldering eyes

As they bend and curve

On undulating walks.

Suspicious, they meditate on mysterious sounds,

And are stunned into

A ruffle of feathers

As winter, warlike, makes an abrupt entrance.

Cracking its whip in the sunglow,

It unveils the harsh finale

To the unfinished song

Of this sweet day.

# ...THESE FRAGMENTARY ROSES

A strong wind sings a song of madness

And rudely scatters the roses that had waited for me like lovers.

As they fall, a moonbeam catches their redness

And turns it into rings around a ghostly moon.

Uprooted petals wrap themselves 'round me wanting to be mended,

And I kneel to rescue them before their beauty ebbs.

I save an armful for a little while

Until they curl up and dry in patterns in the dust.

Long after they disappear,

Their redness echoes in the crimson glow of a descending moon.

Who can unveil the mystery of these fragmentary roses?

And

Why must they die before morning?

# FADING FLOWERS

Summer bolts the door.

And in the morning,

Parched petals shudder and ache with desire

For one last glimpse of blue sky.

There is no solace in chilled sunshine

That sweeps over them in empty gardens.


Where do fading flowers go?

Once connected to the rose,

Once inseparable from the thorn,

Broad-winged petals streak across the sky

To migrate with birds

And race with the wind.


…In celebration of one more spring,

Overlapping petals ride back to earth

On a witty wind that plays the flute.

Huge petals now hang etched like lanterns ablaze

Against the mahogany brown arms of a thin little apple tree.

# TABLEAU VIVANT

The moon emerges from behind a cloud

Wearing a hat with white feathers

That dance over the mimosas

That stand in bunches

Against the briars on my fence.

Is she watching me

This moon with the flapping feathers?

Or is she watching the frog

the rabbit

and the butterfly

Who nervously sleep under her wide eyes

As if being hunted?

# THE SYCAMORE TREE

The more I stare at the sycamore tree,

The more I want to bridge its haunting loneliness,

To dwell within the abyss of its stillness,

To become two selves at one with its calmness,

To breathe when it breathes,

And to listen with its ears when the ghosts of other trees

Speak in the night.

I want to be there when, betrayed by demon winds,

Its leaves become unhinged and fall one by one,

Littering the countryside with red and bronze ruffles.

I would gather and arrange them by color.

I want to be there when, with tiny fussy gestures,

It cradles swallows on its bare limbs

Stretched out like washlines,

Lulling them to sleep with songs

That mingle with the cello-tones of the wind.

# THE LONESOME TREE

What quells the fear of the lonesome tree

When jagged tongues of lightning strike

And thunder beats like a hammer against its heart?

Is it the moon that roams the sky and sits with stars

That bends in the firelight to calm the trembling tree?

The moon she leaves no footprints,

And I do not ask the stars to remember,

But look how now the tree stands like a monarch

Jubilant in the moonlight,

And having cheated death,

Wears diamonds in her hair,

And vows to be a mother to the sleepy swallow

Who makes this tree his home.

# MESSENGERS

Birds rise in the air

Trailing cacaphonous messages

Over quiet waters below.


The sweet meat of

Golden brown nuts

Ripened in a rainfall,

Will bring them joy.

# JUST WEEDS

The sun high in the sky

Shoots rays over weeds

That poke grimy faces up out of stones

Shouting

here we are!

here we are!

# TINY NUT-BROWN SPROUTS

Tiny nut-brown sprouts lap up the rain,

And unpredictably turn into hulking trees

With hard green pears and crab-apples hanging.

Luscious, but pungent and tart to the taste,

They were mine for a day.

I will remember them

Long after they return to the ground as seedlings.

# ...WHILE OUT FOR A WALK IN THE FOREST

A stony-faced moon seems to step out of the sky,

And with soft cat-steps whose tread I cannot hear,

Follows me home.

It dares to enter my window in search of games to play,

And leaves demonic shadows with yellow-green eyes and smiley faces

That stretch and slink around the walls –

Brazen as swaggering lions breathing fire,

While out for a walk in the forest.

# WHAT IS THE TREE...

What is the tree

And will I ever know it?


Unanswered,

I look closely at the magnolia

And it is like looking into the sea.

Noble.

Indestructible.


Blossoms wrought like ivory through wind and water

Set my heart on fire.

Unnerved by their beauty,

I conclude that the great wide arms of the tree

Sprout poetry,

And that the pulsations of its great green heart

Beat just for me.

Just for me.

# A SINGLE PERFECT PETAL

I stand mute before a hundred purple hyacinths.

Fierce lights that burn all night,

Infinitely sweeter than honey are they.

Hard is my heart when I bend to gather them in my arms,

And I weep silent tears for the stems I have broken.

A single perfect petal floats free,

And flies like a butterfly over meadows and forests,

Until wearily, it settles at my feet.

Mystically merging with an ancient stone,

The broadened petal becomes a mighty-throne for a tiny frog

Who sleeps and dreams of ruling in this momentary kingdom.

# MORNING GLORIES

The sap runs high in the month of May,

And all that is left of winter is one snowflake.

Crickets are in the mood to cricket,

And the morning glory can hardly wait to bloom again.

Hypnotic in purple,

Wild blossoms shed winter coats,

And do not seem to be blossoms at all,

For they hang deceptively now,

Like bells billowing from braided vines.

How lovingly they wind themselves in caring curves

Around the wrinkled arms of the old chestnut tree

That sits and broods in sorrow like some banished king –

Raised arms festooned,

No longer naked in the unremitting sunshine.

# THE REGALISTIC VINE

Spawned at the root of a blueberry bush,

A sleeping vine wakens

And, washed by the sun,

Sails across fields of waving blue-eyed wildflowers.

Bowing like a pompous queen,

Her royal highness weaves crowns or viridescent leaves.

Pinning one atop an inscrutable scarecrow lost in reverie,

It becomes a silken perch for a meadowlark,

Who feeling lifted by its touch,

Sings a rapturous solo over and over again,

Tossing humility to the wind

In proclamation of the coming of

This regalistic vine.

# THE CAPERING FROG

Perched in seclusion beneath a canopied leaf
On a tiny river where thick water lilies perfume the air,
A sleepy frog daydreams to the rhythms of the undercurrents
While ogling the crystal beauty of the serene water.
From the depths of his aloneness,
He croons softly to the stained-glass reflections of himself.
A rambling vine of creeping honeysuckle in full plumage
Trembles and listens to the ancient lullaby.
In the white shadow of a moonrise,
The river smiles to hear the song it has heard
A thousand times before.
Scattered dark masks of beckoning trees
Answer with low whistling sounds,
And are content to watch,
As, one by one,
Three stars move out of a deep hollow in the sky
To light this endless night
While, at low tide,
The capering frog performs a delicate dance,
And in sudden linkage with his secret past,
Plunges into the watery abyss of the rising river.

# THIS MYSTIC MOON...

Circling and glittering,

A blank white paper moon looks down over hilltops

And swings like a lantern over villages and farms,

Where roosters crow every morning,

And crickets mimic them at midnight.

Along the way, a thin poplar is etched in its light.

Looking like a scarecrow,

It stands behind an ear of corn that burns like a torch,

And adds a sculptural touch

To the surreal tapestry of the night.

A magnolia, barely touched by the moon,

Sheds petals that patter to the ground like drops of milk.

All the earth is candlelit and seems ready for a coronation,

When, in perfect orchestration with the rising sun,

This mystic moon tiptoes away and disappears.

# TABLEAU

Stung by an icy wind,

Scarlet leaves of autumn shrink and curl

Like scrolls of yellowed paper.

An old tree – so lame, so withered –

Groans and turns its colossal head for one last look

At the lark whose impassioned love song

Engulfs the night.

And in the quiet calm of the sky,

Quivering stars with eyes like diamonds,

Watch a cold cold moon

Slip through the black fingers of the night,

And float like a white balloon leaking bright lunar light

Over mountains and canyons,

Before sinking like a phantom into a hole in the horizon.


Bleak and empty,

The sky is just a sky without the moon.

# GOODBYE BLUEBELLS!

I despise winter

When it reaches down to the roots of my beloved bluebells,

And crushes them with ice.

A budding spring cannot warm them,

And they die in summer.

There they lie cold as marble

With no new buds to shine on me.

Birds call to them and fly in a frenzy,

As if in sorrow.

Goodbye bluebells!

Once they were my passion.

Entwined in my arms,

I beheld their radiant beauty as they unfolded

And bared their soul to me.

I am starved for the sight of them.

# UBIQUITOUS ROSES

Have the roses lost their senses?

Ubiquitous in two shades of red,

They bloom in over-arching heaps of clusters and columns

And gothic spires so tall,

They overshadow the perambulating ivy!

Petals flare open on upraised faces…

Warm and breathing,

Such roses never die.

They could dress kings on thrones

Or be crowns for beggars who lie on barren ground

Dreaming of immortality.

# ...THE LOVELIEST DAY IN MAY

The cursèd sting of winter's fury tears at my walls
And puts a chill on my back,
Before vanishing with a howl down the chimney,
Where it spirals up as a wisp of smoke.
And on the loveliest day in May,
Spring rekindles its flames and enters the world,
Pausing to bring me roses...
One red, one white.
My heart sinks to think they will be brittle and spoiled,
Before I lay the trellis that will cradle them.
Mountain laurel frames my window with fleecy blossoms,
And honeysuckle overruns the bottom of my garden,
Beckoning from many-knotted vines
Where swarms of butterflies flit all day long.
Stretching in unbroken lines,
Multitudes of cawing crows fly up out of checkered cornfields
Once frozen in December's ice.
Thrust into the sunlight,
Yellow-green sheaves flash like emeralds under a sky so blue,
The cornflower cannot match it.
From a deep pocket in the sky,
Rain in all its liquid beauty
Begins to fall in drops like plums that clatter like chimes
Against the spires and cantilevers of my roof.

# BROAD-BILLED BIRDS

Surreal shadows stir in the foggy light of morning,

And spring to life as broad-billed birds.

Ornately costumed in fragrant feathers,

They stare out from wide oval eyes that are full of secrets,

And scurry along a wet beach on tall broomstick legs.

Mimes at play,

They pair off like dancers

To the merry cries of the rag-tag flock.

Gracefully scraping the shell-thin sand,

They leave a frieze of footprints that is soon washed away

By the salty licks

Of the hungry tongue

Of the silent sea.

# SANDPIPERS

Sandpipers with golden crowns
Step softly out of wet hollows
Onto broken shells
Along a lonesome beach.


Poised in calm contemplation,
They find themselves reflected
In the silver mirrors of the sea.
One by one, they smile upon a sea urchin,
Mesmerizing him with the mime and magic of their chorus.


Restless travellers,
Kings in velvet coats,
They waken to catch the sun
And sing a thousand songs
To a thousand moons.
And when the last song is sung,
They close their eyes and
Concentrate on what is meant to be –
…The ecstasy of a bittersweet surrender
To the open arms of a waiting sea…

# OCEANS OF BLOSSOMS

Oceans of blossoms driven by the wind,

Wave goodbye to white clouds that once cradled them.

Swooping down in an uproar of petals and pollen,

They alight on a drove of desolate trees

That stand shivering in cloistered silence.

Majestic monuments battered by time,

Don Juans without passion,

They bend and twist in solemn surprise

And lift melancholy eyes to behold in wonder,

The luminous blossoms that pierce the darkness

And hang like golden parasols

From the crumbling branches of these oddly beautiful trees.

# A SPIDER WHO LOOKS LIKE INK

A spider who looks like ink,

Weaves a large web while never tangling its threads.

Dipping dried insects' wings into the morning dew,

He takes a tiny taste.

Closing his eyes,

He sways on his web,

And dreams of the sweetness of doing nothing.

# IMPATIENT BUTTERCUPS

A playful pool of buttercups,

Impatient to be on the move,

Hurries down a honey-colored hillside.

Petals flutter and peel back,

Folding into bonnets waving in the wind.

Sighs and murmurs punctuate the damp earth,

Enriching it.


Is this the lonesome hour of their brief flowering?

Where are they going?

What enflames their laughing faces?

And what do they whisper when they cling to each other?

# THE DEAD LEAVES OF YESTERDAY

In the silvery mist of morning

Exhileration is everywhere.

Shocks of yellow flowers inhale the freshness

And besiege the garden wall –

Roses – bent but blushing still – in robes of red

– Whisper like lovers.

And forget-me-nots pour forth

Their soul in fragrance that

Spreads like honey

Through trenchant branches of the sycamore –

And through the garden gate

And along the long long path

Where frogs and dusty spiders

Are happy to bathe their feet

In the bright sunshine that has

Found them playing beneath

The dead leaves of yesterday.

# HAUGHTY HOLLYHOCKS

A glassy blue summer sky
Mirrors a corner of a radiant garden
Where double rows of haughty hollyhocks
In ruffled robes of red blossoms,
Meet, like dowager duchesses,
To gossip in the sunshine.

A crinkled caterpillar,
Spawned deep in the shirred center of a brown-eyed weed,
Rests unobtrusively on a broad scalloped petal.
Slowly unfurling to explore its periphery,
He hangs upside down from wispy parallel threads,
And does an impromptu jig on this silken trapeze
To the discordant tune of a frog's croaking.

From slit eyes that seem chiseled.
He sees the piquant hollyhock seeds erupt
And fly into space on a breath of wind.
Enchanted, he looks up at their rapid ascent,
And in an uncanny act of prefiguration,
Changes shape in a wink –
And triumphantly continues as a blithesome butterfly
Conspicuous among the hollyhocks.

# BLUEBELLS ABLOOM

Bluebells abloom
Rustle and whistle in a summer wind
Carving serpentine paths,
They flow like a river
As they sweep across yellow-green meadows,
Chattering and fussing
Like newborn magpies.
The smell of their ripe petals
Cuts through overgrown forests
And comforts a nonchalant owl
Peering out from the hollow of a petrified tree.

And when morning breaks,
Light-hearted swallows with sapphire eyes,
Sing FORTISSIMO!
And desert the sky
Hungry for a taste of the cool nectar
That trickles and spills in globs of white foam
From the countless billowing bouquets of babbling bluebells.

# THE WITCHES' BREW THAT IS MY GARDEN

In the witches' brew that is my garden

The wishing heart finds a sense of order beneath the chaos.

Their silence speaks to me in the fragrance that burns my throat.

A rabbit comes in his loneliness to be by me and the roses.

My breath is balanced

But when he leaps away

I know he is not meant to be mine.

My pulse quickens when by chance

I see a chickadee – the one with the beautiful eyes,

Plundering grapes off the belly of a vine

Whose interlocking branches creak

When transitive winds pass through them.

And when everything has fallen,

And winter comes to freeze the tears of separating lovers,

The tallest tree will turn to ebony,

And part of me will see some splendor yet,

In the brittle leaf that is a secret listener

To the sighing sounds of corpses beneath the muddy ground.

# FORGET-ME-NOTS

# PROMISES

In a yellowy midnight,

Roses in the rain

Repose on canopied thrones

Of intensely blue flowers with orange breasts.

Ferns carved on slender stalks

Capitulate

To large flat leaves floating by

In water whitish with the milky juice

Of water lilies.

All around

Stately shadows

Carved in wood or stone

Gather like lovers with silent secrets

…to taste the splendor of yesterday's kisses

And whisper promises for tomorrow.

# RENASCENCE

I stare at thin little cakes

on a plate

turning sour when you go

This I know…

the time is late

for loving you

and I am cold.

Renascence takes too long.

It takes too long!

# THIS TIME WHEN YOU GO

Cover me with the umbrage of your love.

This time when you go

Passionless in the blazing sun,

There will be shade,

There will be shade.


Embrace me in the full hollow of your arm.

This time when you go

Aloof in the cold thin shaft of dawn,

There will be warmth,

There will be warmth.


Persuade me with the opulence of your mind.

This time when you go

Voiceless in the cadenced flow of light,

There will be dreams,

There will be dreams.

# NOTHING TO SHOW

Dried flower petals

Fragrant yet,

Swim in shimmering rivers.

Restless flames,

Intense. Emotional.

Passion penetrates the snow.

Brilliant lights burn as you go

And I have nothing to show

That you were here…

That you were here…

# WITHOUT HER

Lonesome am I
Since my love
Walked away
To lie
Beside someone else.


Something in her walk
Was different.
No lightness.
In profile
Magnificent was she.
Hair unravelled.
No communication
In her back.


Walked away!
To lie
Beside someone else.
It happened to me.
Different without her
Am I.

# MY DARLING MAUVE FLOWERS

My darling mauve flowers

Spent the winter sleeping

In brittle ground

Preparing for propagation.

Sway gently now!

Sunlight fingers in fissures

Beneath loamy soil,

Moist and rich

Soft and sweet

Loamy soil.


My darling mauve flowers

Arrange their petals now.

Flower buds open ablaze

While the sun holds a lighted match

To their smiling faces.

# CATKINS

Silvery velvet catkins

On pussy willow reeds,

Whisper in low vibrating keys

That they are pleased,

That they are pleased!

# A CHORUS OF DAISIES...

A chorus of daisies,

Asters and dandelions

Sings low beneath loamy soil.

Ribbons of gold humming,

Waiting to strike up the darkness

To the unwritten tunes of tomorrow.

# WHERE I WAIT...

In twisting coiling motion

Plants grow from spicy roots.

Bluish blackish berries glisten

On fat shrubs.

The fragrance of their delicate pink blossoms

Lingers beneath your window

Locked in the dark shadow of the willow tree

Where I wait...

# IF YOU COME 'ROUND AGAIN

If you come 'round again,
I will love you vaguely,
Not so sure this time.
I will love you meagerly,
Keep you from my brain,
Where you exist, persistently.

If you come 'round again,
I will love you blandly,
Not so strong this time.
I will love you thinly,
Leave you waiting in the rain,
While I weep, tearlessly.

If you come 'round again,
We will travel lightly
Share undistinguished love,
Mechanically.

If you come 'round again,
We will sing metallically,
Give unrequited love,
Brokenly,
…if you come 'round again,
O, if you come 'round again.

# MY LOVE'S EYES

I cannot leave my love's eyes.

Precious jewels of emerald green

Are stored there for safekeeping.

And the season for emerald green

Is not yet over.

# ...THAT YOU ARE NEAR

The sun is everywhere
Casting yellow cat eyes on the water.
Clusters of white flowers appear
In the fertile warmth.
Blazing mobiles suspended
Forever timeless
While rivers flow
Mindless, with no place to go.


The sun is everywhere
Casting funny faces on the water.
Red purple and orange plants
Trail sweet-smelling flowers
In the fertile warmth,
Warmth forever endless.


In the shimmering loveliness
The mind needs no persuasion
To know that you are near
...that you are near.

# GOLDEN FLOWERS

Golden flowers

In yellow robes

Of silken luster

Twine and twist

On long thin stems.

Their light-green leaves

Washed in a mist-like rain

Bend downward…

Downward to you.

# DANDELIONS

In the morning

Dandelions greet the sunshine

With great feeling

Squandered in the open field.

Incoming tides of long slender shapes

Move swiftly

In spray

Blown from a rough wind.

Brilliant ornamental runs

Of yellow ribbons unwind…

The palest ones blush into ripening fruit

As my love bends to choose one for her hair.

# THE LONELY ROOM

A lonely room

Waits for me

Where tangled hair

Blooms no more

On my pillow.

# ...EVEN BY STARLIGHT

When summer goes,

She goes completely.

Closes the door.


Earth not sleeping

Yet watchful...

Is unproductive.


Bored with colors dwindling,

Breast cupped to catch the sun,

She spreads thin feathers

Over brown burrows in the ground.

Barren. Monotonous.

...Even by starlight

When I am being loved by you.

# FORGET-ME-NOTS

Face to face

With your eyes

I realize that they are flowers, really.

Forget – Me – Nots.

Not the kind that grow in pots,

But tossed up on a hillside.

Wild clusters of blue,

They remind me of you, nearly.

# WHEN SOME MORNINGS...

When some mornings,

The leaves do not love the tree

As before,

They hiss mournful whispers

And deny the dreams of yesterday.

# BUTTERFLIES

Out of a deep hollow

In the earth's surface,

Seeds scatter

High on the horizon

And burst into butterflies.

# THE COLOR OF YOUR EYES

In a moment of abandon,
Small purple flowers explode
On low-rounded hills,
Softly seeking unrestrained pleasures
In the first hour of day.

Flowering tides flow toward shore,
Small tufts of wool
Billow forth in floods
Of semi-precious stones.
Extravagant. Intricate.
In a showy display
Of densely matted flower heads,
They move impulsively,
From slow to quick,
Gushing out,
Floating free,
Talking wildly.
Encrimsoned by desire,
They surge in spirited dance.

The clove scent of wall flowers
Leads me on –
(Sharp intolerable spice)…
And falls on stones the color of your eyes.

# THE BUTTERFLY

Stay awhile.
Poor butterfly,
Bits of colored glass in flight,
You desert the sky
Too soon.
All nature is inconsolable.

What artist painted you?
Impugn him for such brazen purpose!
There is no voice as sweet as yours,
And yet, you have none.
Dazzling in the sunglow,
You go – in haste,
Perhaps in rage, to die.

Flowers crowd 'round,
Flirt flagrantly in the sunshine,
Toss petals at you in the wind.
Roses raise flamingo faces to the rite.

O brilliant patch of color
Danse Macabre is your solo.
As you streak the drab stone
With brilliant tracery,
All nature vivified,
Cries out against the stingy stipend
Of your brief tomorrow.

# CHILDREN OF THE MIST

Children of the mist,

Flowers coiled at spring's door

Pierce the darkness

Blooming in many shades of lavender.


Fluttering like flames

In stiff and crowded confrontation.

Passionate. Breathless.


Love dies hard beneath my window

In flowers the will not come again.

# FORGOTTEN FRUIT

When sweet red winter apples come,

They chill the flaming ardor of the peach.

Seeds of apricot, plum and cherry

Shine hard on vines

That once were sea-green.

O lustrous gems

Scattered in a winter sky,

You are not easily forgotten!

Apples the color of purplish wine

Compel the dandelion to say little.

The loganberry swims in honeyed satisfaction,

Yielding moisture to the arid ground.

Stones of forgotten fruit

Listen underground,

Waiting to be found

In time to taste fermented juices of one more spring.

# YOUR FACE ELUDES ME

Your face eludes me now,

When once I could have carved it

In the snow – from memory,

That face is somewhere else now,

When once it graced my pillow,

Lived within my elbow.

Your face eludes me now,

When once I could have fit it

Into blue pieces of sky – from memory.

That face is somewhere else now,

When once it gave crescendo to antique waltzes

Danced daily, while my life

Chased it along avenues of my mind.

Your face eludes me now,

When once I could have kissed it

In the mussed up grass – from memory.

# FIREFLY

In the dark most silent night,

Stars rush out to greet the firefly.

Small bright light without flame,

Flashing dance of green fire,

Floating wingless she-bird among blue shadows,

What seeest thou?

Singing sometimes,

She ignites the unloved stone with mounting desire

And goes alone to celebrate,

A voice forever alive

That waits on stars…

In the dark most silent night.

# STARS

Stars.

Diadems of light

In a treeless forest

Ignite the night.

# WINTER LOVE

Winter love
Keeps through the cold season,
Adorns earth's sweet swelling curves
Monotonously.
What kind of plumage
Dwells in tones of blue green and gray?
The sycamore stiffens in cold ground,
Unyielding…
Birds that sing in evening
Muse on memories
Of creamy white flowers
Spun with blue-black berries.
The vine that climbs with hissing noise
From candied roots
Greets the winter artist
In a sputtering light
As he struggles to extract pure purple from his palette.
Underground stems tremble
In midnight cold
And taste your nearness
In a thin bundle of leaves
Blown about by the wind.

# IN A MOMENT OF MADNESS

In a moment of madness

Pale red flowers

Return to life

As small purple plums.

# WHITEFACED WEEDS

Without invitation

Whitefaced weeds

Usurp the ground

From more desirable plants,

Thrusting upward

Among broken stones.

They yield a soft light,

A feast of lanterns

Ready for gathering.

# JACK-O-LANTERNS

Jack-O-Lanterns.

Brilliant torches,

Shimmering flames in a fiery night.

Kingly crowns

That dazzle for a little while.

# CONEBEARING TREES

Splashed by sunlight,
Conebearing trees
Make their way
Scattering red berries
From dark green juicy leaves.

In lonely places
The wind plays the Queen,
Blows her horn,
Squanders priceless seeds
With great tenderness.

A blade of grass
Colored yellow by the sun,
Tapers to a point.
Its length
Extends upward  to brighten the night when it comes.

The trees are wet.
Blown about,
They catch the wind
(Withered leaves remain attached
Whispering refusals…)
And wait
With unbearable grace,
For the oncoming loneliness of tomorrow.

# PROMENADING FLOWERS

(Sad little) flowers promenading in a field,

Lean on the wind,

Throw red faces

At the sun.

Yellow throats

Caught on hollow stems

That cannot run.

Helpless, they have no place to go…

…no place to go.

# SEPTEMBER FLOWERS

September.

Flowers break into shivers,

As cool air flows across

Their faces.

Petals rise.

Wingless butterflies

Freed in the noonday sun,

Melt together.

Red, yellow and orange ribbons

Spread out to sea.

Their odor runs over me…

Intoxicating.

Chilling.

# DUET

The young tree moves in agitation

To arrange her hair made perverse by gnarled nests.

Long fingers lift lovingly to unlace knots

In strands whose color was borrowed from your eyes.


The young tree moves in exultation

And combs her hair twisted by cantankerous birds.

Amorous arms rise commandingly to restore calm

To the last movement of our duet.

# SALLY AND BOB

Only the trees remain to remember
Sally and Bob
Who graffittied their names on my wall
Last September
SALLY LOVES BOB.

Where are they now, I wonder?
Sally and Bob.
BOB LOVES SALLY.
Lost, I hear their voices vibrate in leaves that fell
Last fall.
Near my wall.

They lived for a day.
Wore crowns.
Sally and Bob
Whirled in the wind,
Danced on birds' wings,
Had last flings!
Sally loved Bob.
Suspended between wall and sky,
Images staring into loneliness,
They never meant to die.
Sally and Bob.
Bob and Sally.

# COMMON AS CABBAGES

# ECHOES OF MY CHILDHOOD

# GRANDMOTHER

Blossoms on the vine,
Cradle songs remembered,
Lullabies recalled.
Skin crinkled like crepe…
She was the flame,
The sentinel who guarded us,
The cupbearer,
The ancient monument,
The flinty heart,
The mitigative influence,
The ethereal fluid flowing in from the stars.
We were flowers clustering around her,
She was the river that enfolded us,
The steady ray of light that shone,
The brilliance that flowed sweetly over us.
Innocent as a meadow plant, her face appears in the morningstar.
Her nearness is a gift at daybreak
That twines itself into just-born leaves.
Her nearness in space exists in the passage of time
Between two full moons.
She is the perennial plant –
Flawless as a buttercup.
Hers is the voice that floats out over rivers
We never got to know.
She is disguised in the hard wood of trees,
Sweet-smelling pine and birch.
Redolent of sage and smoke…
She is the capstone on our hearts.

And we who are all alone,
Hunger for her love.

# JOEY

The smell of rain.
A quiet night.
"Come closer to me little Joey,"
Whispered the Spectator…waiting.


What did we dread in dreams before sunrise?
Listen!
Melodious singing of the nightingale comes before tomorrow.
Small bright lights in the sky burning all night.
You are the one, Little Joey, little life.
One… Two… Three… Three years.
He longed for more.
Died in the cradle.
Washed away on little cold feet.
A whirring noise, the doorlatch opened.
In a single long step
The Onlooker lifted the listless child and took him on painted pony.
Away without a whisper.
Pompous four-legged animal followed us all
But took Joey.


What was there about him?
Eyes.
Glowing pieces of coal,
Smoldering pendants.
Luxuriant growth of hair rich and extravagant,
Lustrous along the neck.
Skin double smooth.


The sky turned red like a flame.
We could not think of sleep.
The sun was a lamp that lit the streets as we searched.
Good morning.
Light blue ribbons woke us with a delicate touch.

(Birds stepped gracefully on shallow waters
Along the shore where sand was unstressed and easily crumbled).
Burdened with grief and sorrow,
No longer buoyant,
We sought the constant playmate we had lost.

Menace to little children,
Close to us all, Thief on nimble feet!
Death took our Joey.
Joe Vida!
Embraced and took him on painted pony…
Over a hill.
Desolate, we searched the ruins of our tiny street.
Turned it upside down.
Is it real that he died?

Joey!
You were so sweet and we never said goodbye!
We never said goodbye…

# GRANDFATHER

When Grandfather comes to our house,
It is a real celebration.
We hang around the kitchen,
Give up the outside world,
And wait for this elder statesman,
This man of all seasons.

Every ritual is suspended.
We who are natural born explorers
In a wilderness of weeds
Whose names we cannot know,
Sit on chairs and wait.
What an experience of frustration and suffering!
On this day
We sacrifice uncharted walks down uncharted paths,
But the sacrifice fits like a glove.
A mantle of pleasure we wear
When Grandfather hoves into sight.

My father brings him.
Grandfather would get lost if he had to travel alone
To an alien town.
We tremble to think of Grandfather lost in a labyrinth
Of train and trolley car changes.
Too complicated!
Better go get him
And bring him straight in the car.

Grandfather! Grandfather!
We run, we jump.
Go to him, get to him, get to him.
Be first!
(Why do I love him so much?)
Shapeless pants.
We sit in his lap.

He begins to show the watch and chain for which he is famous.
Heavy gold watch
With miraculous cover that opens and closes,
Opens and closes, mechanically.
Listen!
This watch ticks forever…
Goes everywhere that Grandfather goes.
Oh would that I were that watch!


Time. Time.
"You have time for Grandfather, little children?"
"Yes, we don't go out anymore today.
We stay to worship at your feet."


The face is set in a smile
Different from all other smiles
For the dimples it makes in the cheeks.
Grandfather has the most profound dimples,
My father says so.
This rarity in our Grandfather is part of the endearment.
We hold him in high esteem and behave like regular sports
In front of him.
We swagger…
"Tell me little children."
He wants to hear everything,
And we let loose!
He doesn't miss a thing.
Each child receives equal attention.
He is fair.
What a Grandfather!


Time to go.
Oh no!
Okay.
He stays for another cup of coffee
With tablespoons of sugar.
Bread and butter, too.
"Children… Children… Come here."

Our hearts beat fast.
We know what comes next.
The suspense is killing.
Now!
A large black leather purse with three compartments appears
Bulging with silver.
Grandfather acts like a rich man.
Coins heavy in his pocketbook.

To each child he gives a quarter.
"And what will you do with so much money?"
"Buy shoes for school,"
We say every time.
"Good, good."
He is pleased.
Dimples showing.
Oh what a Grandfather!

Now he is leaving.
"Goodbye, Goodbye.
Come again next time.
Come again next time.
We will wait, we will wait…"

We race to the candy store
To spend the windfall.
Old Mr. Starke treats us with new respect
As we order like swells
…a penny's worth of this,
Two cents worth of that…
We want everything.
The world is ours.
Inflation comes to impoverished egos.
The glass case contains precious colored gems
That rest in little trays.
We buy extravagantly.

Salt comes in the mouth to spoil the taste of the candy.
I am weeping.
I forgot to tell Grandfather that I love him,
I grieve for the lost moment
When I was struck dumb.
Voiceless,
I didn't say it… I didn't say it…

# COMMON AS CABBAGES

At four I was a handful.
I had cast my lot with ruffians,
Lechers, loudmouths.
We loped along in lopsided association
From sunrise to sunset.
Leaping, running, galloping,
We plundered, stripped, spoiled.
Moving in long swinging strides,
We trimmed trees, cut branches,
Twigs and stems.
Sometimes enjoying edible fruit…

Loveless, not rich.
Ours was a low diet
Lacking in cultivated taste.
Ill-mannered,
Crude beggars with a broad sense of comedy.
We invented burlesque,
Slapstick, farce,
And racy dialogue.
Told absurd, improbable stories.
Talkative, dreamy, forgetful,
Braggadocios.
Common as cabbages.

# RUNAWAY

The circus! The circus!
What magic the circus holds
For all of us.
The charm of it.
The circus weaves a spell
From which few can escape.
Children of all ages
Have dreamed of running away from home
To become – Animal Trainer – Trapeze Artist
Or Clown.
A child who has been to the circus
Is willing to give up the comforts of home,
Parental love, friends, education –
All in exchange for
The glamour of life as a Rover
In the company of – Elephants
Tigers – Monkeys – Bears – Ponies and Lions.

Take Tommy.
Here he was at the ripe old age of ten
Running away from home.
He had to join the circus!
The smell of sawdust
The spot-light in the rings
The swinging trapezes
The animals – the clowns –
The applause – the music blaring –
The circus sights sounds and smells
Held him in their spell.
This was his destiny –
The circus life.

He would tell them he was older than ten.
They would believe him
Because he was big for his age,

And they would give him a job as Animal Trainer.
He wanted to be with the animals
Because he had a way with them.
Instinctively animals responded
To Tommy's touch
To Tommy's voice.

His only worry about leaving home
(And it was a big worry now) –
Was Bingo.
What would Bingo think if he knew
Tommy had deserted him for the circus –
For other animals to take <u>his</u> place
In Tommy's heart?
Bingo would be jealous and hurt.
He would be sad-eyed and mopey,
Never again to wag his tail with joy
At the sight of Tommy.

With these thoughts racing through his mind,
Tommy began to question the rightness
Of what he was doing –
Joining the circus.
He knew suddenly
That there was nothing right about deserting
The best friend he had ever had.
Good old Bingo –
They were pals,
And no one deserts a pal.
Bingo was the best dog
In the whole world,
More valuable than
Tigers – Lions – Elephants – Horses -- Monkeys.

Tommy turned homeward filled with love.
He knew Bingo would be waiting
And wondering.
He began to run…

# THE LETTER

She awoke this morning feeling
A special day was in the air.
The sun had risen while she slept
And she was grateful for the golden glow
Which filled her room.
She felt like shouting her joy at being alive
On this perfect spring day.
A feeling of expectancy made her hurry.
She decided not to waste a single moment.
She was ready to greet
This miraculous day!

The beauty of the morning rushed in
Nearly choking her
Leaving her breathless.
Was it all real
Or had someone assembled
Sky – trees – flowers – birds
And arranged them in perfect landscape
While she slept?
Familiar sounds were all around –
Scurrying – flitting – flying.
Creatures of all shapes and sizes
Going about their business in noisy fashion.
She stood motionless
Not wanting to disturb any of the pieces
In the brilliant tableau.

And who had invaded the far end of the garden?
A truly infrequent visitor –
The shy rabbit himself!
So absorbed was he in twitching his nose
And in itching his fur with a long hind paw,
That her presence didn't frighten him away.
But as she held her breath,

The front gate creaked,
The magic spell was broken,
And the rabbit hopped away.
"Here comes the old mailman,"
She thought,
"With a bag of nothing for me"
But what was he saying?
"A letter for me, really?"
Suddenly…
She realized what the large white envelope must contain.
It was a letter
From the boy who had captured her heart!

Oh,
Let this keep on being the perfect day
She implored the trees – the flowers – the birds.
Let him want me –
I couldn't bear rejection today.
With nervous fingers
She destroyed the envelope
And as she read the letter addressed to her,
She knew that this was the most perfect part
Of an already most perfect day.

"Yes! Yes! Yes!"
The letter was alive with verbiage composed by
This sweet laureate.
He wanted her as she had wanted him…
The boy who had captured her heart!

# POETIC ESSAYS

# DO I REMEMBER HIM?

"Do I remember him?"
"Yes – I remember him."

"He still inhabits my mind – my dreams. I am restless for the sight of him and so I look up at the sky – searching in the unusual formation of clouds for a particular shape. But my dreams for any physical resemblance to him are crushed by the phenomenon of two perfectly paired birds flying romantically by – going who knows where?"

"This chain of events is interrupted when the telephone rings and I am reminded that life begins all over again all the time. But then I realize that something terrible happened to me. What was it?"

"For the past ten minutes I have thought about him and only him. Almost joyfully I think a terrible trick has been played on me. Curious – I rush to find him. Sure enough, he's there in the lamplight and laughingly he starts to tell me the same story he told me only yesterday. Suddenly, he doesn't say anymore. Wanting his attention I sink into his arms where I remain trapped by the illusion of happiness when he kisses me and kisses me and kisses me…"

"–To be continued…"

# CRISIS

Gordon –

Your phone call was wonderful.
There you were as I remember you – poised – elegant –
radiating charm. You warmed up the moment.
Everything has changed. But as the French would say –
"The more things change – the more they remain the same."
As I approach the future – I approach the past.
What happened?
We added up to a collection of exquisite moments.
Entwined lives fused with passion.
Casting a backward glance – I observe our performances
more like playacting in a failed movie – or were they
revelatory moments in real life? Or were they figments
of my imagination?
I think about you all the time.
Your capacity for decision
(you chose the wine.)
The things that happened to us.
The people we were.
The stuff we did.
It was lovely all the time.
I can hardly bear to recall the ending.
Shattered glass.
And then a stillness.
It made me sad for a long time.
But now on a winter's night I feel a surge of happiness
when I think of spring and how the apple trees will be
singing and how a gust of wind will bring the smell of
apple blossoms into my life once more.

# DEAR FRIEND

One of the luxuries of life is finding a friend like you.

Your lovely card came like an April breeze

Blowing over me on a day when fallen leaves danced endlessly –

Leaving a sense of loss.

Your words of comfort and good wishes are intense –

All encompassing –

And bring a sense of renewal into my life.


May the happiness of today last and shine on you always

As tho' a star.

# THINKING OF YOU

I think of you in so many ways.

For the broad sweep of your brilliant mind.

The clear light you shed on crucial detail.

Your gentle humor and incomparable style.

I am grateful for the staunch support you always gave.

It was a joy to have you all those years.


My love for you runs deep.

And you will always be my umbrella in the rain.

# YEARS

Thank you for the years —

As I work hard to consume their blessings

I will connect them with

The wonderful flavor and taste of love

You have given me.

# EROS

Down with whatever it is that Cupid does!

And you can take the moon

And give it back to the Viennese.


Let us never be too busy to know that trust

Is for children in school

And that caring makes fools of us all.

# LET'S LUNCH!

I was so surprised to see you recently

That I almost forgot to breathe.

Seeing you struck a chord of memory,

Yes – after all this time

I remember you as I remember the tree

That stands like an open umbrella beneath my window.

We meet again and the conversation seems routine.

Does my nonchalance mask something?

Am I split in the heart over you?

Not at all.

But I distinctly remember a first – rate evening

When this "upper-class" girl

Dined out with an "upper-class" guy.

Is it real that we ever did this?

What dream is this?

Let's not dream.

Let's make things better.

Let's lunch!

# THE HEART

The heart is battered to bits

When it does not hear from you.


I cannot just abandon you as a memory.

I must find out what happened.


–The heart is slow to learn.

# COMMUNICATION

Like the silent "b" in "doubt", you are silent.

This excites my curiosity.


Something that is puzzling or inexplicable stimulates me.

A saying, a question, a picture containing a hidden meaning,

Invigorate me.

A person who is enigmatic, mysterious in anyway –

Kindles my intellectuality and ignites my feelings.


To understand music and art is to understand

That pauses are followed by new beginnings,

That space is filled with motion, energy and light,

That nothing is absolute–

Not even the emotional connections between people.


Pauses and silences always precede great revivals in

Art, music and literature.

Similarly, between persons,

Pauses and silences create the suspense

That intensifies the renascence when it comes.

# REFLECTIONS

Someone I knew a long time ago reminded me of the willow tree that stands aloof under an autumn sky. I had watched that tree grow and change leaving its young self behind. And as if in a mirror, I could see this woman in its reflections. Everything the tree could do – she could do. She could be calm and strong and quietly beautiful. She did not perceive herself as a tree nor even as beautiful. But any man with a liking for green eyes would have died a little to meet her.

Now nothing interests a man so much as falling in love – to be animated by someone who would change the way he looked at things. Love is almost too mysterious to contemplate. But it does have infinite potential for self-realization. This man – this Mr. XYZ – was needing more. Something was missing from his life – but also he was needing to be free.

But let us go back to the lady with the green eyes. Hungry for someone who would know what she wanted – some spark of recognition from Mr. XYZ – some point at which he and she would be shedding new light on her life – and in the long run bringing some pleasure.
A magical thing would happen.
They would sing the same songs.

So here is Mr. XYZ.
Eager lover – he would turn to her as to an old book which he adored – feeling the urge to read and reread it - losing himself in it – putting aside his life – undefined as it was – to know himself better.

And yet – watching himself with a sense of ironic detachment he saw hero and heroine entwined with no passion.
Worlds apart.

But having capitulated to her sexuality which was compounded by the haunting mystique of those green eyes – he was astonished at the colossal boredom which confronted him in the morning when the world was stirring.

Why pretend?

If he died she would not miss him.

He wished he had never met her.

His back ached.

His head swam and he was furious with himself for already he was reminiscing about her kisses.

The feel of her lips was still on him.

A delicious pain pulsed through his limbs and he gave himself up to the fruitless thought that he didn't care a damn about her.

His heart was filled with a sense of liberation that calmed him.

It was Sunday.

The morning was grey.

To his surprise the sun broke out.

He wanted a small whiskey.

Far off in the distance he could see a café.

Suddenly – the way she smiled came back to him.

Would this never end?

What had really happened?

What was the truth?

Had he been derelict in not finishing something he had started?

Carefully, he put his feelings away.

"Let's get drunk" he said to a pigeon who flopped down at his feet and waited.

Both shivered as our hero walked quickly away without turning back.

# YOU

Like an unexpected song

You will always come back to me

Like a gentle wind

And will remain in my memory

As my life's golden moment.

# EDITOR'S NOTE

Sadly, in 2008, my mother Mitzi Libsohn passed on, leaving as her legacy a gorgeous and eloquent collection of poetry which she had written over a thirty-five year period. Her ultimate desire was to have that poetry – her precious and cherished life's work – published in book form. That was her dream. Regrettably, however, that was not to be. Overwhelmed by her loss and stricken by grief, I was determined to fulfill that dream – it became my grand obsession. I began the slow and painstaking process of lovingly arranging and editing her manuscript, persevering – never wavering in my devotion – for I was committed to the ideals of my mother. The result of that devotion is her book "Immortal Kisses - Confessions of a Poet," completed in the way I believe she would have wanted. Now she has her dream - it has come true.

My mother will be greatly missed by all whose lives she touched – especially by me to whom she leaves a legacy of wisdom – careful advice – devotion – and much love of the deepest kind.

PAULI ROSE LIBSOHN

# DAVID